AFRICAN AMERICAN
TRAILBLAZERS IN
CIVIL RIGHTS

T.M. Moody

African American Trailblazers in Civil Rights
African American History for Kids, #5

Copyright © 2024 T.M. Moody

Paperback ISBN: 978-1-961437-08-1
Ebook ISBN: 978-1-961437-09-8

Kulture Kidz Books
Tymm Publishing LLC
www.tymmpublishing.com

Author: T.M. Moody
Editor: sadeknows
Illustrations: johangerrar
Cover and Interior Designer: TywebbinCreations.com

Contents

Introduction

Have you ever heard the word "trailblazer"? Do you know what it means? A **trailblazer** is someone who does something that no one has ever done before. In **African American Trailblazers in Civil Rights**, you will learn about many people who fought for equal rights for all people.

What are **civil rights**? Civil rights are the rights that a country's government gives to its citizens. Everyone should be treated equally, regardless of race, religion, or other differences. These rights may include having the right to vote in elections or getting a good education at a public school.

This book has three sections. Let's learn about each section below.

1-Early Civil Rights Movements (1865-1954)

The struggle for civil rights in the United States has been going on for a long time. Some of the early movements took place in the late 18th to early 19th century. You're going to learn about people involved in the abolitionist movement and the women's suffrage movement.

2-Civil Rights Milestones

The official Civil Rights Movement in the United States started in the late 1940s and ended in the late 1960s. African American people were not allowed to attend the same schools, restaurants, and many other places that were labeled "White only." This was known as segregation. African Americans grew tired of being treated unfairly. You will learn about milestones or important events during this time.

3-The Civil Rights Movement (1954 - 1968)

Meet the "Big Six"– the six civil rights leaders who played an important role in the American civil rights movement. You will also learn about organizations and the organizers behind the scenes.

PART 1

EARLY CIVIL RIGHTS MOVEMENTS (1865-1955)

Chapter 1

Abolitionist Movement

Slavery is a system where people are owned by other people. They're forced to work and are treated like property. Some people were against this system, and they were called abolitionists. An abolitionist is a person who fights for slavery to end. This was done through the abolitionist movement. The **abolitionist movement** was an organized effort to end the practice of **slavery** in the United States. This movement would lead to a war later known as the American Civil War.

The **American Civil War** was fought between two groups of people. One group wanted to keep slavery, and the other group was the abolitionists. The people who wanted to keep slavery were mostly from the southern states and were called **Confederates**. The other group was called the **Union** and was mainly from the northern states. Fighting between the two groups started in 1861 and lasted for four years.

On January 1, 1863, President Abraham Lincoln signed an important document called the **Emancipation Proclamation.** This document stated that all enslaved people in the Confederate states had to be set free. It would take over two years for this to happen. There weren't phones or the internet back then, so messengers traveled on horseback to bring important news.

On June 19, 1865, Union soldiers arrived in Galveston, Texas, and told the enslaved people the good news. This was the last group of enslaved people in the United States. June 19 was the official end of slavery and became known as Juneteenth. Juneteenth became a national holiday in 2021.

Meet some of the African American leaders during the abolitionist movement.

Frederick Douglass (1818-1895)

Frederick Douglass was born into slavery as Frederick Augustus Washington Bailey in February 1818. He didn't know the exact date of his birth, but was born on the Eastern Shore of the Chesapeake Bay in Talbot County, Maryland. Despite Frederick's difficult start, he bravely escaped to freedom at the age of 21.

Frederick didn't enjoy his freedom quietly; he spoke out against slavery. He told people about the unfair and harsh life he had experienced as an enslaved person and encouraged them to fight against it.

He didn't stop there. Frederick started a newspaper called "The North Star." This newspaper helped share important ideas about freedom and fairness. Imagine trying to make your own newspaper without computers or the internet!

During the Civil War, Frederick worked hard to recruit black soldiers for the Union Army. He believed that everyone, regardless of skin color, should have the chance to fight for their freedom and rights.

In 1889, something remarkable happened. Frederick Douglass became the U.S. Minister to Haiti, which made him the first African American to hold such a high position in government. This was a big deal because it showed that anyone, no matter where they started in life, could achieve great things.

Sojourner Truth (1797-1883)

In 1797, Sojourner Truth was born as Isabella Baumfree in Swartekill, Ulster County, New York. In 1827, she escaped from her master, who had unfairly sold her five children to different owners. Can you imagine how brave and scared she must have felt running away?

She found safety with a kind Quaker family. **Quakers** are a group of people who believe all people are unique and equal. Since they believed no one should be harmed or threatened, many Quakers were **abolitionists**, people who worked to end slavery.

The Quaker family helped Isabella in a court case to bring one of her sons back to her. This was a big deal because it was rare for an African American woman to win in court during those times.

After gaining her freedom, Isabella changed her name. She chose "Sojourner" as her first name because she traveled across the land, sharing important messages with people. Later, she added "Truth" to her name to show she always wanted to speak the truth – that enslaved people deserved to be free.

Standing over 6 feet tall, Sojourner was a commanding presence. When she spoke, people listened. Even though she never had the chance to learn to read or write, she had a natural gift for inspiring others with her words,

making her a legendary speaker and abolitionist.

Harriet Tubman (1820-1913)

Harriet Tubman, known as the "Moses of Her People," was a heroic leader who guided many slaves to freedom. She was one of the most courageous conductors of the Underground Railroad, a secret network that helped slaves escape to free states.

Harriet was born as Araminta Ross in March 1822 in Dorchester County, Maryland. In 1844, Harriet faced a tough decision. Her master had died, and she heard the slaves might be sold and separated from their families. Knowing this, she decided to escape to freedom. Although she started her journey with her brothers, they were too scared and returned home. But Harriet was determined and continued alone.

As an Underground Railroad conductor, Harriet was very careful and always made sure that the people she helped escape slavery were safe. She was known for her clever disguises and secret messages that helped guide her passengers on their journey. Harriet used to say, "I never ran my train off track, and I never lost a passenger," which meant she helped everyone to safety.

There was a big reward for catching her, but Harriet was smart and always avoided capture. She helped many people, including her own family, find freedom and a new life.

Imagine...

Imagine standing in a crowd, listening to Frederick or Sojourner speak with passion about their experiences as a slave. How do you think their words would make you feel?

Imagine being as brave as Harriet, leading and helping so many people on the Underground Railroad! How can you help people in your life?

Chapter 2

Women's Suffrage Movement

In 1870, the **Fifteenth Amendment** was passed, and African American men were given the right to vote. This was an important amendment because many states had laws that prevented African Americans from voting. This amendment made it illegal to deny someone the right to vote based on their race or color.

However, the Fifteenth Amendment only gave African American men the right to vote. Women were not given these rights. So, a new cause was born—the **Women's suffrage** movement. This movement fought for a woman's right to vote in elections. After a long fight, on August 18, 1920, the Nineteenth Amendment was passed, giving women the right to vote.

Despite the Fifteenth and Nineteenth Amendments, it would be hard for African American men and women to exercise their right to vote until the 1965 Voting Rights Act.

A set of "laws" known as **Jim Crow** made it hard for African Americans. State and local governments created their own laws, which pushed for segregation. **Segregation** is setting one group of people apart from another group. Most of the time, African Americans were treated unfairly.

Despite the conditions, African American women leaders from the women's suffrage movement continued to fight. They fought for two reasons:

(1) To have equal rights and to be treated fairly for being African American.

(2) To have equal rights and to be treated fairly for being a woman.

Frances Ellen Watkins Harper
(1825-1911)

Frances Ellen Watkins Harper was born free in Baltimore, Maryland, in 1825. Her parents died when she was young, so she was raised by her uncle and aunt. They made sure she got a good education. After studying at her uncle's school,

Frances became a teacher and writer. Later, she would become an **abolitionist**, like the people you met in the previous chapter.

Frances wrote poems and gave speeches asking for the end of slavery. She traveled and talked to many people about why slavery was wrong. Harper also spoke about equal rights for women and helped founded the **National Association of Colored Women Club (NACWC)**.

When she published her first novel, *Iola Leroy* in 1892, she became one of the first African American women to write a novel.

Ida B. Wells Barnett (1862-1931)

Ida B. Wells Barnett was the most famous African American woman journalist of her time. She was born into slavery as Ida Bell Wells on July 16, 1862, in Holly Springs, Mississippi. Despite her early years, it didn't stop her from getting an education.

After earning degrees from Rust College and Fisk University, she taught in Memphis, Tennessee, and began writing articles for the Black Newspaper, *Free Speech*. She also wrote articles for the *Memphis Watchman*, *Detroit Plain Dealer*, *Indianapolis World*, *Little Rock Sun*, and many others.

During Ida's time, many African Americans were lynched or severely harmed for unfair reasons. The people who died didn't even get a chance to show they were innocent or to have someone listen to their side of the story in court. Ida and so many others lost loved ones this way.

Ida worked hard to make sure people knew about it through her writings. She would eventually speak across the United States in major cities and even travel overseas to Great Britain to spread the word about the injustice of lynching.

Ida also spoke up for women's rights and was a founder of the **National Association of Colored Women Club** (NACWC).

Mary Church Terrell (1863-1954)

Mary Church Terrell was born to well-to-do parents and attended a private school in Ohio. She graduated from Oberlin College with her bachelor's degree in 1884, making her one of the first African American women awarded a college degree.

Mary was a part of the group that founded the **National Association of Colored Women Club** (NACWC). The group included some women already introduced in this book, like Harriet Tubman, Frances E. W. Harper, and Ida Bell Wells-Barnett.

Mary became the first president of the NACWC and gained national attention for her fight for women's suffrage and racial inequality.

All three women came together to form an organization in 1896 that supported women's rights. The National Association of Colored Women Club is still active today. Did you know Mary and Ida would join forces with others to help create one of the oldest and largest civil rights organizations? Find out more in the next chapter.

Imagine ...

Imagine being able to write a letter or an article about something you were passionate about or wanted to see change. Both Frances and Mary used the power of the pen to fight injustice. How do you feel when others read your writing?

Chapter 3
NAACP

The **National Association for the Advancement of Colored People** (NAACP) was founded in 1909 by a group of black and white citizens committed to social justice. It is the nation's largest and strongest civil rights organization.

Throughout this book, you will find many civil rights trailblazers who were members of the NAACP. Let's meet some of the founders and leaders.

W.E.B. Du Bois (1868-1963)

Born William Edward Burghardt Du Bois on February 23, 1868, in Great Barrington, Massachusetts, he became a famous teacher, writer, social scientist, and one of the founders of the NAACP.

A **society** is a big group of people who live in the same town, city, or country. They can share similar things like rules, traditions, and ways of doing things. A society can also be how people work together, help each other, and follow rules so everyone lives well and safely.

Du Bois loved to teach about African Americans. He studied how they lived and were treated in America and would later write what he learned in a book called "The Souls of Black Folks."

He also worked as the editor of a magazine named "The Crisis," which was part of the NAACP, an important group fighting for the rights of black people. In this magazine, he wrote about important issues black people faced in the early 1900s.

Mary McLeod Bethune (1875- 1955)

In 1904, with only $1.50, Mary McLeod Bethune founded a school for girls in Daytona Beach, Florida. Bethune held the school in an old house next to a city dump with five little girls and her four-year-old son. By 1923 the school became Bethune-Cookman College, and had 600 students, 32 faculty members, and an $800,000 campus free of debt.

After the women's suffrage movement (we talked about that in the last chapter), Bethune continued to encourage women to register to vote. She took part in many organizations. In 1924, she served as president of the National Association of Colored Women's Clubs. In 1935, she became the founding president of the National Council of Negro Women. In 1940, she became vice president of the NAACP. She remained in this position for the rest of her life.

Imagine ...

Imagine if you lived during the early 1900s. Would you have joined the NAACP? Why or why not? What role do you think you could have played?

PART 2

CIVIL RIGHTS MILESTONES

Chapter 4

Brown vs. Board of Education of Topeka

Years ago, in the United States, schools were separated by the color of the students' skin. This meant that white children and black children went to different schools. Sometimes, children like Linda Brown from Topeka, Kansas, had to travel a long way to go to school even though there was a school (for whites only) near her house.

This would all change with a very important case called Brown v. Board of Education of Topeka. This case represented Linda and students in other states, like Delaware, South Carolina, Virginia, and the District of Columbia.

In 1954, the Supreme Court, which is the top court in the United States, said that separating schools by skin color was not fair. They decided that all children, no matter their skin color, should be able to learn together in the same schools. This would begin desegregation, a huge step in making sure everyone was treated equally.

Let's meet two lawyers on this big case.

Thurgood Marshall (1908-1993)

Judge Thurgood Marshall was a lawyer and Civil Rights leader. He worked for the NAACP. One of the biggest things he did was win a court case called Brown versus Board of Education. Marshall would go on to even bigger things after this great win.

In 1967, Marshall was appointed Justice of the Supreme Court by President Lyndon B. Johnson. This made him the first African American ever appointed to the Supreme Court.

Supreme Court Justices serve lifetime appointments or for the rest of their lives. Marshall served for twenty-four years before retiring in 1991.

Constance Baker Motley (1921-2005)

A civil rights lawyer, Constance Baker Motley became well known for her work on Brown versus Board of Education. She worked alongside the future Supreme Court Justice, Thurgood Marshall.

Judge Constance Baker Motley became the nation's first African American woman to serve as a federal judge in 1966, when President Lyndon B. Johnson nominated her. She served in the U.S. District Court for the Southern District of New York.

Motley not only served in the judicial branch, but also served in the legislative branch. In New York, she became the first African American woman in the state Senate. She also served on the executive branch on a local level when she became the first woman to be elected as the Manhattan Borough president.

Imagine...

Both lawyers, Thurgood Marshall and Constance Baker Motley, worked together on this important case. Imagine you are interviewing one of them about their work. What questions would you ask?

Chapter 5

School Desegregation Begins

Desegregation was a hard road and involved many brave young people. School desegregation began when the law said children of different races had to attend the same schools. Now, this should have been helpful for all students so they could learn about each other better. But not everyone liked this idea, even though it was now a law.

Let's meet some people and students involved during school desegregation.

Daisy Bates (1914-1999)

Daisy Bates was born Daisy Lee Gatson on November 11, 1914, in Huttig, Arkansas. Remember, we talked about the NAACP in the last section. There are groups or chapters of this organization in cities, towns, and states. When Daisy Bates was older, she would lead the Arkansas group of the NAACP.

Daisy and her husband started a newspaper called *The Arkansas Weekly*. This newspaper told stories about how people fought for equal rights.

In 1957, Daisy helped nine African American students go to a school that only white students used to attend in Little Rock, Arkansas. These students were called the Little Rock Nine.

Top Row: Minnie Brown, Elizabeth Eckford and Ernest Green

Middle Row: Thelma Mothershed, Melba Pattillo and Gloria Ray

Bottom row: Terrence Roberts, Jefferson Thomas and Carlotta Walls

On the first day, the nine students tried to attend Central High School, but they faced a tough situation. As they approached the school, a large crowd of angry people shouted at them. There were police there too, but instead of helping the Little Rock Nine enter the school, they blocked them from going in. This was a scary situation! How do you think the students felt?

Their first attempt to enter the school gained national attention. President Dwight D. Eisenhower stepped in to make sure the students could safely enter the school. Eisenhower sent federal troops from the 101st Airborne Division to Little Rock. With the protection of the troops, the Little Rock Nine could finally enter Central High School on September 25, 1957, and attend classes.

James Meredith (1933-)

James Meredith was born on June 25, 1933, in Mississippi. He was the first African American student to attend the University of Mississippi, also known as "Ole Miss," in 1962. James had fought for his right to study at there. He had to be protected by the police and soldiers because some people didn't want him at Ole Miss. His courage helped start changes so that other colleges and universities would be open to everyone, no matter their race.

Imagine ...

Imagine being the first to start at a brand new school in the face of angry mobs. What gives people the courage to stand up for what's right, even when it's scary?

Chapter 6

Montgomery Bus Boycott

There are many ways people can fight for change, and a **boycott** is one of them. A boycott is when people decide not to buy or use something because they want to change something about it.

The Montgomery Bus Boycott was a big event in American history that happened in 1955. It started in Montgomery, Alabama. Before the boycott, buses in Montgomery had an unfair rule. African American people had to sit in the back of the bus, and if the bus was too full, they had to give up their seats to white people. The boycott was meant to change this.

Rosa Parks (1913-2005)

Rosa Parks was the secretary for the Montgomery chapter of the NAACP. On December 1, 1955, Rosa was tired after a long day, but she also was tired of the unjust bus rule. She refused to give up her seat to a white person. Because of this, she was arrested. Her courage made many people in Montgomery decide to **boycott** or stop using the buses.

The boycott lasted for more than a year! During that time, African American people in Montgomery walked, rode bikes, or shared rides instead of taking the bus. It was a peaceful way of protesting.

Finally, the leaders of the boycott, which included Martin Luther King Jr., won their fight. The laws were changed, and the buses in Montgomery became fair for everyone. People could sit wherever they wanted, no matter their skin color.

The Montgomery Bus Boycott was one of the important milestones in the fight for equal rights in America. Rosa Parks (1913-2005) is often called the Mother of the Civil Rights Movement.

Imagine...

Imagine you lived in Montgomery and were part of the bus boycott. What would that year have been like for you and your family? How would you have managed without using the buses?

PART 3

THE CIVIL RIGHTS MOVEMENT (1954-1968)

Chapter 7

The Big Six

The "big six" were a group of civil rights leaders who played a key role in the American civil rights movement of the 1960s. They worked together to organize and lead many of the important civil rights events, like the March on Washington and the Selma to Montgomery voting rights marches.

Martin Luther King Jr. (1929-1968)

Southern Christian Leadership Conference (SCLC)

Born on January 15, 1929, Martin Luther King Jr. grew up to be a very important leader who fought for equality and justice. After graduating from Morehouse College in Atlanta, Georgia, in 1948, he became a pastor like his dad and granddad. He married Coretta Scott in 1953, and they had four children: Yolanda, Martin III, Dexter, and Bernice.

Dr. King believed in peaceful protests. A **protest** is when a group of people gather together to show that they don't like something or want to change it. They usually hold signs, chant slogans, and march to let others know about their feelings or concerns.

There are other ways to fight for change, like a boycott. We learned about the boycott in the previous section when Rosa Parks refused to give up her seat on the bus. What you did not know was that Dr. King led the Montgomery Bus Boycott.

In 1957, Dr. King became the leader of a group called the Southern Christian Leadership Conference, or SCLC, for short. The SCLC organized some really big events like the Birmingham Campaign in 1963, where they did peaceful protests in Birmingham, Alabama, and the Selma to Montgomery marches in 1965, where people walked together to fight for the right to vote.

One of King's most famous moments was when he gave a speech called "I Have A Dream." This happened on August 28, 1963, during a big march in Washington, D.C., where he spoke to about 250,000 people.

Sadly, King's life ended when he was killed by James Earl Ray in Memphis, Tennessee, in 1968.

To remember his great work and life, the United States began celebrating his birthday as a special day called Martin Luther King Day. This holiday happens every year on the third Monday of January, starting from January 20, 1986.

John Lewis (1940-2020)

Student Nonviolent Coordinating Committee (SNCC)

John Lewis was born on February 21, 1940 in Troy, Alabama. He was a civil rights leader, minister, and politician who was a leader in the Civil Rights Movement. He was brave and always stood up for what he believed in, even when it was difficult or dangerous.

He went to college at Fisk University and the American Baptist Theological Seminary. After college, from 1963 to 1966, he led a group called the Student Nonviolent Coordinating Committee (SNCC). This group worked peacefully to make sure everyone, no matter their skin color, was treated the same. He is also one of the "Big Six" leaders who helped to organize the March on Washington.

In his later years, John became a member of the United States Congress. He was elected to the House of Representatives in 1986 and continued to serve until his passing in 2020. John Lewis served 33 years as a public servant.

James Farmer (1920 – 1999)

Congress of Racial Equality (CORE)

James Farmer was born on January 12, 1920, in Texas. He started a group called the Congress of Racial Equality, also known as CORE. CORE also believed in peaceful ways to fight for civil rights.

One of their most famous actions was the "Freedom Rides" in 1961. These were bus trips through the southern part of the United States to protest against the unfair treatment of black people. Activists of all races rode on the buses together to show that everyone should be treated equally.

A. Philip Randolph (1889-1979)

Brotherhood of Sleeping Car Porters

A. Philip Randolph was born on April 15, 1889, in Florida.

He was best known for organizing a labor union called the Brotherhood of Sleeping Car Porters. A **labor union** is a group or team of workers who work together to make things better in their jobs. Often, these groups may want to be paid fairly or want to make sure their workplace is safe for everyone.

Randolph fought for fair pay and better working conditions for black workers. The Brotherhood of Sleeping Car Porters became the first African American labor union to sign a contract with a major American company.

He also played a big role in the civil rights movement. One of his most famous achievements was organizing the March on Washington in 1963, with Dr. Martin Luther King Jr. and the other "Big Six" leaders.

Roy Wilkins (1901-1981)

National Association for the Advancement of Colored People (NAACP)

Roy Wilkins was born on August 30, 1901, in St. Louis, Missouri. He attended the University of Minnesota and graduated with a degree in sociology in 1923. After college, he worked as a journalist and editor for various African American newspapers, including the *Kansas City Call* and the *St. Paul Appeal.*

In 1955, he became the executive director of the NAACP. Roy held this position for over 20 years until he retired in 1977.

Roy like many other civil rights leaders, believed in using peaceful ways to make change. During his time in the NAACP, he fought against segregation and for the rights of African Americans. He along with the other leaders in this chapter, helped organize the March on Washington for Jobs and Freedom.

He also played a key role in advocating for the Civil Rights Act of 1964 and the Voting Rights Act of 1965. Both of these laws helped make changes for African Americans.

Whitney Young (1921 -1971)

National Urban League

Whitney Young was born in Shelby County, Kentucky, in 1921.

He attended Kentucky State University and graduated with a bachelor's degree in social work. When World War II happened, he served bravely in the U.S. Army to help protect his country.

In 1961, Whitney Young began leading an important group called the National Urban League. This group worked hard to make sure that everyone, no matter the color of their skin, had an equal chance to get good jobs and be treated with kindness and fairness.

Whitney Young not only worked alongside the leaders in this chapter, but also with famous leaders like President John F. Kennedy and President Lyndon B. Johnson. Through his work with the Urban League, Whitney was able to help push for new laws that made changes for African Americans.

In 1969, people were so impressed with Whitney's great work, they suggested him for the **Nobel Peace Prize**. This prize is a pretty special award that people get when they have done great things to make the world a better and more peaceful place. It's named after a man named Alfred Nobel, who wanted to give awards to people who help others and bring peace. This award is given out every year.

Even after Whitney Young passed away, his legacy lived on. In the year 2000, President Bill Clinton gave him a special award called the Presidential Medal of Freedom to recognize and honor all the amazing work he had done throughout his life.

New Laws

There were two new laws created after the many marches and protests during the Civil Rights Movement:

(1) Civil Rights Act of 1964

This law said everyone in the United States should be treated equally and fairly, no matter the color of their skin. Places like restaurants, schools, and stores couldn't say, "You can't come in here because of your skin color." It also made sure that everyone had the same chances for jobs and could vote in elections.

(2) Voting Rights Act of 1965

The Voting Rights Act of 1965 was a new law that said everyone, especially African Americans, could vote in elections without any problems. Before this law, some people made it difficult for African Americans to vote by using unfair rules and tests.

Imagine...

How would you feel if you lived during this time and found out about these new laws?

Chapter 8

Organizers

We met the top leaders of the civil rights movement in the last chapter. Even though the leaders may be out front, there are people behind the scenes whose work is just as important.

Let's meet some of these organizers and the organizations they served.

Ella Baker (1903–1986)

Ella Baker began her involvement with the civil rights movement as a field secretary in the NAACP. Later, she served as a director for different NAACP branches from 1943 to 1946.

In 1957, Baker co-founded the Southern Christian Leadership Conference (SCLC) alongside

Dr. Martin Luther King Jr. and other civil rights leaders. She served as SCLC's first executive director.

Baker's most important role in the civil rights movement was helping to create the Student Nonviolent Coordinating Committee (SNCC) in 1960. SNCC would organize **sit-ins**.

Imagine if you and your friends went to a restaurant, and you weren't allowed to sit at a table or in a certain area just because of how you look or the color of your skin. That would be really unfair, right?

In the sit-in, students would peacefully sit down in the area where they weren't allowed and refuse to leave. Many of these students were arrested, but the sit-ins helped people see how wrong segregation was and helped bring about important changes.

Julian Bond (1940–2015)

Julian Bond was born in Nashville, Tennessee. He grew up to become a strong advocate for civil rights. Julian also helped form the Student Nonviolent Coordinating Committee.

Later, he pursued a career in politics in Georgia. In 1965, he was one of 11 African Americans elected to the Georgia House of Representatives.

In 1971, Julian helped create the Southern Poverty Law Center (SPLC) in Montgomery, Alabama. The SPLC was like a law firm that protected people from unfair rules and made sure everyone was treated with kindness and respect, no matter what they looked like or where they came from.

He also taught at various universities, sharing his knowledge and passion for social justice.

Septima Poinsette Clark (1898–1987)

Septima Poinsette Clark was born on May 3, 1898, in Charleston, South Carolina. She grew up to be an amazing teacher and civil rights activist.

When Septima was looking for a teaching job, Charleston didn't hire African Americans to teach in its public schools. In 1916, she found a teaching position in Johns Island, South Carolina. In 1919, Septima returned to Charleston and taught at the Avery Institute. While teaching, she joined the NAACP to encourage the city to hire African American teachers.

Septima's involvement with the NAACP gave her a chance to work with Thurgood Marshall. In 1945, the two worked together on a big case that fought for equal pay for black and white teachers. Septima received a big salary increase when the case was won.

Unfortunately, in 1956, South Carolina made it illegal for public employees like a teacher to belong to civil rights groups like the NAACP. Septima refused to stop her work with the NAACP and lost her job.

In 1961, Septima joined the SCLC (founded by Martin Luther King Jr) as its director of education and teaching. She remained at SCLC until she retired in 1970.

Medgar Evers (1925 - 1963)

Medgar Wiley Evers was born on July 2, 1925, in Decatur, Mississippi.

After serving in World War II, Medgar attended Alcorn College (now Alcorn State University) in Lorman, Mississippi.

In February 1954, Medgar applied to the University of Mississippi Law School, but his application was rejected because of his race.

Medgar began working with the NAACP on a lawsuit against the school. Thurgood Marshall was Medgar's lawyer. They didn't win the case, but a few months later, in May 1954, the famous *Brown v. Board of Education* case would make sure blacks and whites attend schools together.

Medgar became the first field secretary for the NAACP in Mississippi. As state field secretary, he traveled around Mississippi asking people to join the NAACP and register to vote. Soon, Medgar would become a well-known civil rights activist.

Sadly, Medgar and his family received threats because of his activism. In May 1963, their house was firebombed. Only a few weeks later, Medgar lost his life when he was shot in the driveway of his home.

Fannie Lou Hamer (1917 – 1977)

Fannie Lou Hamer was an African American civil rights activist and leader in the 1960s.

She was born in 1917 in Mississippi into a family of sharecroppers. **Sharecropping** was a hard life where farmers had to give the landowner a portion of their crops.

In 1962, she was inspired to join the civil rights movement after attending a voting rights workshop.

She went on to become an influential leader in the Mississippi Freedom Democratic Party, an organization she helped found to challenge the state's all-white delegation to the Democratic National Convention in 1964. Throughout her activism, she spoke out against racism, police brutality, and other forms of injustice.

She was a prominent figure in the Selma to Montgomery voting rights march of 1965 and is remembered for her powerful oratory. Hamer was a strong advocate for the rights of African Americans, and her legacy remains alive today.

Dorothy Height (1912- 2010)

Dorothy Height was born on March 24, 1912, in Richmond, Virginia.

She was a smart student but was denied being able to attend Barnard College because of her skin color. She would later attend New York

University and earn a bachelor's and master's degree in educational psychology.

Dorothy worked as a social worker in Harlem and would start her civil rights journey at the Harlem Young Women's Christian Association (YWCA). She would eventually become the president of the National Council of Negro Women (NCNW) in 1957. Dorothy served as president for over four **decades**. A decade is ten years, so Dorothy served over forty years. While she was president, she focused on many things, including making sure people registered to vote.

Dorothy's civil rights work impressed people like Eleanor Roosevelt, President Dwight D. Eisenhower, and President Lyndon B. Johnson.

Jessie Jackson (1941 –)

Reverend Jesse Jackson was born Jesse Louis Burns on October 8, 1941, in Greenville, South Carolina. Adopted by his stepfather, his last name changed from Burns to Jackson.

Jesse began his leadership journey while he attended the Agricultural and Technical College of North Carolina in Greensboro. He majored in sociology and took part in civil rights protests. He would later join SCLC and worked alongside Martin Luther King Jr.

He became involved in politics in the 1980s. He then ran for president in 1984 and again in 1988 under the Democratic Party.

He founded the Rainbow/PUSH Coalition, a social justice organization that continues to fight for equal rights and opportunities for minorities today.

Bayard Rustin (1912 - 1987)

Bayard Rustin was born in 1912 and raised by his grandparents in West Chester, Pennsylvania. He grew up learning about **Quaker** values of nonviolence and peace. Quakers believe all people are unique and equal and many were abolitionists.

After serving in various organizations, Bayard met A. Philip Randolph, who would later become his mentor. A **mentor** is like a wise friend who helps you learn and grow.

In 1941, Bayard became a part of a group that pulled together plans for the March on Washington. The goal of the march was to protest the discrimination of black workers in the defense department. That march never happened because President Franklin D. Roosevelt signed an executive order that opened up jobs for black workers.

Bayard also fought for gay rights, which sometimes discouraged others from working with him. But years later, the idea of a big March on Washington came back up again. Bayard worked with Martin Luther King Jr. and others to organize the 1963 March on Washington.

Even though he passed away in 1987, President Barack Obama awarded Bayard the Presidential Medal of Freedom for his civil rights activism in 2013.

Malcolm X (1925–1965)

Malcolm X was born Malcolm Little in Omaha, Nebraska, on May 19, 1925. He committed various crimes and was sent to prison in 1946. While he was in prison, he joined the Nation of Islam. He also changed his last name from Little to X.

After he was released from prison, he became one of the most important leaders in the Nation of Islam for twelve years. Malcolm X's ideas were different from other leaders of his time because he talked about self-defense and pride in being black. He became disappointed in the Nation of Islam and left the group in 1964.

Some disliked that Malcolm X left the Nation of Islam, and he received threats because of this. On February 21, 1965, he was killed in New York City.

Chapter 9
After 1968

The Civil Rights Movement is often thought to have ended in 1968. However, the struggle for civil rights has never ended and continues even today. Let's look at two other major movements.

Black Power Movement

1960s and 1970s

The Black Panther : All power to the people.
Library of Congress Control Number 2015649365

The Black Power Movement happened in the 1960s and 1970s. African Americans continued to stand up for their rights and wanted to show everyone that being black was something to be proud of.

SNCC had been active during the Civil Rights Movement, focusing on nonviolent protests like sit-ins. With a new leader, Stokely Carmichael, SNCC changed direction. Carmichael made the phrase "Black Power" popular. He wasn't the only leader during this period.

Huey P. Newton and Bobby Seale founded the Black Panther Party in 1966. Known as one of the most famous black militant political organization, this group created the Free Breakfast for Children Program since many poor children went to school hungry. The free breakfast program started in January 1969 in Oakland, California, and quickly spread. Later, the federal government picked up what the Black Panther Party started and began providing free breakfast across the nation.

Another organization during the Black Power Movement was the Nation of Islam. We learned in the last chapter that Malcolm X was a prominent leader in the Nation of Islam until his departure from the group in 1964.

Black Lives Matter Movement

(2013 -)

Three inspiring women started the Black Lives Matter (BLM) movement - Alicia Garza, Patrisse Cullors, and Opal Tometi. They formed BLM after a black teenager named Trayvon Martin was killed, and the person who did it wasn't held responsible. This made many people very upset. The movement states that black people's lives are important and they should be treated fairly by everyone, especially by the police.

The BLM movement continues today. After a man named George Floyd was killed in 2020, the movement stretched beyond the United States, spreading all over the world. People held peaceful protests, held discussions, and even made art.

Timeline

Early Civil Rights Movements (1865-1954)

1865 - Juneteenth, the end of slavery in the United States

1870 - Fifteenth Amendment passed, giving African American men the right to vote

1920 - Nineteenth Amendment passed, giving women the right to vote

1909 - NAACP founded

Civil Rights Milestones

1954 - Brown v. Board of Education Supreme Court decision ends segregation in public schools

1955 - Rosa Parks and the Montgomery Bus Boycott

1957 - Little Rock Nine integrate Central High School in Arkansas

1962 - James Meredith integrates the University of Mississippi

The Civil Rights Movement
(1954 - 1968)

1963 - March on Washington and Dr. King's "I Have a Dream" speech

1964 - Civil Rights Act passed

1965 - Selma to Montgomery marches and Voting Rights Act passed

1968 - Assassination of Dr. Martin Luther King Jr.

Glossary

Several vocabulary words were introduced throughout the book. Below you can find a review of definitions and also how to say the words out loud. Some of these are great words to know if you are ever in a spelling bee!

Abolitionists (a-buh-li-shuh-nuhsts) – People who worked to end slavery.

Boycott (boy-kot) - When people decide not to buy or use something because they want to change something about it.

Civil Rights (sih-vil rays) - The rights that a country's government gives to its citizens.

Heritage - The history, culture, and traditions that come from your family or country.

Labor union (lay-bur yoon-yuhn) – A group or team of workers who work together to make things better in their jobs.

Legislators (leh-juh-slay-trz) - Members of a body that create laws.

Protest (proh-test) - When a group of people gather together to show that they don't like something or want to change it.

Quakers (kway-krz) - Believe all people are unique and equal and many were abolitionists.

Sit-in - Students would peacefully sit down in the area where they weren't allowed and refuse to leave.

Segregation (seh·gruh·gay·shn) - Setting one group of people apart from another group. Most of the time, one group was treated unfairly.

Sharecropping (shehr-kraa-puhng) - Farmers had to give the landowner a portion of their crop.

Women's suffrage (wim-inz suh-fruhj) – The right of women to vote in elections.

Bibliography

Find the bibliography for this book at https://thekulturekidz.com/bibliographies/

Activity Book

Do you like coloring or puzzles? Be sure to check out *African American Trailblazers in Civil Rights Activity Book*. The activity book includes over 30 activities like coloring, word search, crossword puzzles, mazes, and more.

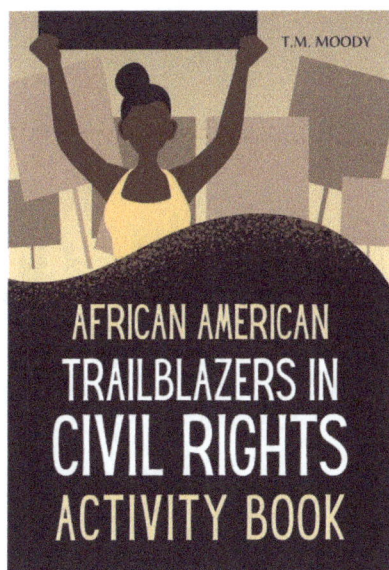

T.M. MOODY

AFRICAN AMERICAN
TRAILBLAZERS IN
CIVIL RIGHTS
ACTIVITY BOOK

About the Author

T.M. Moody has a deep love for history and started the Kulture Kidz website in 1999. She has worked over twenty years as an education content creator and digital curator in public media. Her specialty is creating interactive, standards-based content for the K-12 community.

Moody also has been an author for over ten years. She writes mysteries under her real name, Tyora Moody.

Kulture Kidz Books

Kulture Kidz Books creates content and books for ages 6-12. Our mission is learning about people who made a difference. Visit us online at TheKultureKidz.com.